AF413535

Rightly Wed
& Groomed

RIGHTLY WED & GROOMED

BLISS, BLISTERS, BLESSINGS

PASTOR WALTER 'SPERE' LEWIS

Note from the Author

When I first set out to write *Rightly Wed & Groomed*, I never intended to produce a long book filled with theories or polished philosophies about marriage. My only aim was to tell our story — honestly, humbly, and from the heart — that someone, somewhere, might find hope for their own.

What you hold in your hands is not a grand volume of many chapters and countless pages, but a condensed journey of thirty-seven years lived between two imperfect people who chose to keep walking together under the perfect hand of God.

Marriage, to me, is not so much about the length of time but about the lessons learned. It is about how love grows through laughter, survives through pain, and deepens through faith. These pages may be few, but they are full — full of real moments, both tender and trying, that shaped us into who we are today.

So, if this book feels brief, I invite you to read it slowly. Let each chapter speak to you, let each reflection stir thought, and let each prayer become your own.

May it strengthen your commitment, rekindle your affection, and remind you that even when love seems to falter, grace can make it stand again.

It is my humble prayer that Rightly Wed & Groomed will bless hearts, heal wounds, and inspire couples everywhere to believe that marriage is still a sacred gift worth honouring, nurturing, and celebrating.

With gratitude,

Pastor Walter *"Spere"* Lewis

Linden, Guyana

"This is the Lord's doing; it is marvellous in our eyes."

— *Psalm 118:23 (KJV)*

Acknowledgments

With deep gratitude and humility, I pause to honour the many individuals whose presence, encouragement, and support made this book a reality.

To my (late) beloved wife, Shelburn *"Shelly"* Lewis—this book is as much yours as it is mine. You have been my inspiration, my partner, and my reason to write. I dedicate Rightly Wed & Groomed to you in surprise, but more so in love.

To Mrs. Michelle Bristol-Noble and Pastor Mona Burton—thank you for listening, for believing, and for encouraging me to take the first step in telling this story. Your words were a spark that ignited a long-awaited flame.

To my aged mother, Dorothy Lewis—thank you for raising ten of us with unwavering strength and love. You lost your husband—our father—far too early, yet you never let bitterness take root. I never saw you quarrel or fight with him, and that left a lifelong impression on me. Your example has shaped my ideals of peace and resilience in marriage.

To Joycelyn Croal, thank you for giving me your beautiful daughter. Because of you, this love story was made possible—you are part of it, too.

To all the married couples connected to us, whether in our family, our church, or our community—you are the silent threads that hold this story together. May you find your own reflection in these pages, and may your marriages be enriched by what you read.

To Praise Tabernacle Church, Fruits of Calvary, and all who supported the Reignite the Fire—Fan the Flame initiative, you helped to shape the vision behind this book. Your celebration of love encouraged its telling.

To my children and grandchildren, your lives continue to teach me about legacy and love. You are part of this journey, always.

I am also grateful to Pastor Kelvin Pelle and the family of believers of Casada Gardens Fellowship of Believers Church in Antigua for your support in making this project a success.

Finally, to the One who has held us through it all—our Lord and Saviour Jesus Christ—this work is for Your glory. Thank You for making us a living testimony of Your grace and faithfulness.

Table of Contents

Chapter One
Bliss

"He that findeth a wife findeth a good thing,
and obtaineth favour of the Lord."

– Proverbs 18:22

There's a special kind of joy that can only be found in the early stages of love—a strange mix of butterflies, awkwardness, laughter, bold prayers, and sweet surprises. My story with Shelly began long before I even knew it, as I would later discover that love sometimes grows while you're simply trying to get your life together.

After surrendering my life to Christ in 1981, I poured myself into the things of God. I was young, on fire for the Lord, and—if I'm honest—maybe a little full of myself. I had this idea that zeal made me special. I learned quickly, however, that pride doesn't mix well with grace. Still, I loved Jesus deeply, and He never let me go.

I wasn't the outgoing type, not really. But I did seem to draw attention. Young Christian women began to notice me, much to my surprise. I wasn't sure if it was the fact that I had some decent looks, or maybe it was the seriousness I had about my faith. Either way, it led to a few early entanglements—some of them well-meaning, others, not so wise. I came to realize that I didn't want to continue in relationships that dishonoured God or lacked direction. So, I made a bold declaration to myself and before God: "The next woman I pursue, I will marry."

Enter Shelly.

Before I knew the Lord, I used to hang out at a home where a woman named Joycelyn lived. She was a lively character, well known in the community, and had a daughter named Shelly—school-aged at the time. I noticed the way the guys in the area spoke of her. Shelly was the kind of girl who turned heads, though she didn't live with her mother and mostly passed through. I, being a bit on the shy side, kept my observations to myself. But I saw her— oh, I saw her.

Fast-forward about five years. I was now a committed Christian, trying to live right, and on one ordinary afternoon in the neighbourhood, I heard someone call out, *"Spere!"* That's my nickname, by the way. I turned around and to my utter surprise, it was Shelly. I acted like we were old friends just catching up, trying not to show the mental cartwheels going on inside my head. She had grown into a beautiful, poised young woman, and to my amazement, she too had gotten saved. Not only that—she was a Sunday School teacher!

We talked. She said she needed help with some teaching aids for her Sunday school class—she had somehow heard I was good with art and craft. It was like a scene out of a storybook. Before the day ended, we had agreed to pursue a relationship. Just like that. It felt natural, as if something that had been waiting in the background had just stepped into the light.

I began visiting her home regularly, where she lived with her grandparents, aunts, uncles, and eventually her mother, Joycelyn. I was warmly received. Her family was full of life and laughter. They affectionately called me *"Brother Spir,"* and I quickly learned how much joy a large family can bring. They had a go-to evening dish called shine rice—a low-cost Guyanese dish, but for them it was a high-love meal that stretched to feed a houseful. Let me tell you, I never turned down a plate of shine rice. Never.

But I had one lesson to learn early. Joycelyn, known by nearly everyone (including me) as *"Full Mouth"* because of her lively personality, was no longer to be addressed as such—at least not by me. One of the uncles gave me a look and a stern word when I casually used her nickname. From then on, she was respectfully *"Aunty Joycelyn"* or *"Aunty J."*

As our relationship deepened, so did the laughter and memories. I once told Shelly how long I had been watching her from a distance before we met, and she burst into laughter, shaking her head in amusement at the quiet young man who'd been secretly observing her years before.

There was one night I'll never forget. My church was holding a crusade, and on the final night, the preacher — Pastor Ignatius Phillips who would eventually become Shelly's good friend, decided to let the Holy Spirit take him on a preaching marathon. The service started at 7 p.m.— but we didn't leave until nearly 1:30 a.m. Shelly, who'd attended, sat beside me the whole time, quietly exchanging worried glances as the hour crept on. As we stepped outside at the end of the service, we saw her mother and some family members arriving—armed with a big stick, no less! They were coming to look for her, fearing the worst. Thankfully, the entire congregation was just leaving the church building at the same moment, proving beyond doubt that we had been in the Lord's house all along. Talk about divine timing! I had never wanted such a long sermon again in my life.

When I told the family I wanted to marry Shelly, they were thrilled. Some joked that I'd have to write an official letter requesting her hand in marriage. That I was more than happy to do, so I did. I wasn't about to miss my chance.

The wedding was unforgettable. We planned it a year in advance and chose her birthday—June 18, 1988—as our wedding day. That way, we could celebrate her birthday and our anniversary together (and if I was lucky, even Father's Day, too). The church was filled with well-wishers, and the reception was a joyful, spirit-filled celebration. The leading gospel band at the time, Revival Players, played live music, and even my unsaved co-workers left saying it was the best Christian wedding they'd ever attended. There were food, laughter, music, and love in the air. The honeymoon may have been in a humble rented apartment, but for me, it was a palace—I had my queen, my bride, and we were off to a grand adventure.

Shelly was sweet, with a warm smile that could melt tension, and hair that framed her face like grace itself. She walked with poise, and somehow—even in a crowded church—you could always spot her. I often joked that she had several striped dresses in different colours, so I never had to guess whether she was around.

One day, while working with a navigational crew along the 65-mile Demerara River—servicing lights that guided ships carrying bauxite and other cargo—I came across an orange farm near one of our posts. As the crew picked and ate oranges, one particular orange caught my eye. It was nearly ripe, hanging proudly with its stem and a perfect leaf still attached. I didn't just pick it—I claimed it. "This one is for Shelly," I thought. I carried it carefully, like a gem, and when I gave it to her, she beamed with joy. "Where did you get this?" she asked. I smiled and told her. It wasn't just a fruit—it was love, growing quietly, and finally ripened.

In that season, life was simple. Love was loud even when we said little. We weren't perfect people, but we had a perfect God writing our story. Looking back now, I know—those were just a portion of our days of bliss.

Reflection

"Every good and perfect gift is from above, coming down from the Father of lights."

— James 1:17

Prayer

Lord,

Thank You for the way You orchestrate love stories in the quiet corners of life. Thank You for Shelly—for her laughter, her strength, and her smile that still lights my world. May every couple who reads our story be reminded that You are the best matchmaker and that love—when rooted in You—can weather every storm.

Amen.

Chapter Two
Blisters

Marriage, they say, is like a garden—it must be watered, weeded, and watched with care. But there were times in our journey when it felt less like a garden and more like a battlefield. If the early years were bliss, then the middle years gave us blisters—raw, throbbing reminders that love must often walk through fire to be purified.

We had just come down from the mountaintop of wedding bells and Revival Players, and life was now whispering in a far less melodic tune. The honeymoon didn't stretch far. In fact, it ended somewhere between the kitchen and the sitting room of our small rented apartment. Life was now being paid for in monthly rent and grocery lists.

I took a job I was far too proud to refuse. You see, I wanted to prove something. I had told myself I could be a light in dark places—specifically among other Christians whom I thought weren't shining bright enough. Pride, in a well-dressed suit, whispered to me, *"Go show them how it's done."*

I walked in confident. I walked out compromised.

What I thought would be a mission turned into a mirror. The very sins I judged others for, I fell into. It wasn't a slow descent either. It was as if I had stepped on a spiritual oil slick and tumbled headfirst into temptation. I didn't stop loving God, but I was bruised, ashamed, and bitterly disappointed in myself.

And it didn't stop at work.

Two years into our marriage, I looked at my wife—this woman I had once longed for from riverbanks and orange groves—and I felt...nothing. Love had drained out of me like water through a cracked jug. We fought often—sometimes over real things, sometimes over who left the toothpaste cap off.

When I got quiet to avoid a quarrel, Shelly would jab me in the head with her fingers, determined to provoke a reaction. One day, I reacted. I slapped her. Instantly, I was filled with regret. She didn't deserve that—not Shelly, not the strong woman who cooked my meals, even shine rice with joy and smiled like the sun was on her side.

Another day, during an argument, she picked up a knife—not to use it, I knew that—but in trying to take it from her, I nearly lost my index finger. The scar is still there. A reminder. A memorial. Not of the violence, but of how close we came to letting everything fall apart.

I began flirting with other women. I crossed lines I should have burned. It was Christian misconduct in bold letters. And yet, somehow—through God alone—we never separated. Shelly was firm, committed. Despite the pain, despite my failings, she kept reaching for reconciliation even when I was cold and distant. She loved me even when I wasn't being lovable.

She didn't stop praying. She didn't stop believing.

We had our first child—a boy. Then came our daughter. Later, we fostered three girls, adding both chaos and joy to our home. I wish I could say I turned around quickly, but I didn't. I was like a man stumbling in fog, groping for the love I once felt, trying to convince myself that it could be revived.

I began to pray—not with eloquence but with desperation. I knelt at the side of our bed, whispering through tears, *"God, please give me back that love for my wife."*

And He did.

Not all at once, but gradually. Like the tide returning to the shore of the Demerara River, I so much enjoyed during my younger years. The arguments didn't disappear overnight, but love returned with a softer voice. I began to see her again—not just as a woman I lived with, but as the woman I once watched walk past my work with those favourite striped dresses.

Life began to blossom again. We bought a home, then a car. I had dreams of spontaneous drives and rekindled dates. But often, after long days at work, those plans wilted on arrival. I came home too tired to go out. Shelly, ever full of life, would lament that we weren't doing enough to keep the flame alive. She was right. Still, she endured. She gave herself to teaching—not just in church, but in the classroom. Long nights, test papers, tired eyes.

Then came May 2005.

A sudden illness struck her down—a cerebral aneurysm. We rushed her to Trinidad, to Mt. Hope Hospital. She lay unconscious for more than three weeks in that hospital. Every day, I sat by her side, waiting, praying, fearing. One day, as I stepped into the elevator to leave her bedside, tears escaped my eyes. I felt like I had seen her alive for the last time.

It crushed me.

But God, in His mercy, raised her back. It was a miracle. When she opened her eyes again, the sun seemed brighter. The air is sweeter. The love deeper. The blisters we bore weren't gone—but they had healed into scars that told a better story.

Today, I know what it means to be married to a strong woman. A woman who walks through fire and still smiles. We have two children, and through the years, we've nurtured others as if they were our own. She stood by me through my ministry, through our storms, through seasons of sickness.

In late 2024, we were hit again. A diagnosis: breast cancer. Yet, even now, she is full of laughter and life. We're both older, both facing our own physical challenges, but we're still holding hands, still serving God, still believing that He who began a good work in us will be faithful to complete it.

Blisters are not the end of a marriage. Sometimes, they're the proof that we kept walking.

And I thank God we did.

Reflection: Grace in the Blisters

"Three times I pleaded with the Lord to take it away from me. But He said to me, 'My grace is sufficient for you, for my power is made perfect in weakness.'"

—2 Corinthians 12:8–9 (NIV)

Marriage doesn't just reveal who your partner is—it reveals who you are. And often, that revelation isn't pretty. Pride, impatience, selfishness, and brokenness all rise to the surface in the pressure cooker of committed love. But even in the ugliest of moments, God doesn't walk away.

This chapter of our lives reminds me that love is not just an emotion—it's a decision wrapped in sacrifice, sealed in covenant, and sustained by grace. We both failed. We both wept. But God—merciful, patient, and wise—never stopped weaving redemption into our story.

Like a wound that turns into a scar, our blisters have become testimonies. Testimonies that love can heal. That forgiveness is stronger than offense. That marriages can come back from the brink when God is in the centre.

If you're reading this and feel like your marriage is somewhere between shouting matches and silent rooms, take heart: God still speaks into broken places. He doesn't just restore—He transforms.

Prayer: Through the Blisters

Father,

Thank You for walking with us through every fire, even the ones we lit ourselves.

When we were tired of each other, You waited with love.

When we hurt one another, You offered grace.

When we fell, You didn't condemn us—you lifted us.

Thank You for a love that goes beyond the wedding day, for a Savior who stays through the storm, and for a Spirit who softens hard hearts.

Lord, heal every hurting couple reading this.

Restore what has been lost.

Let them see each other again—truly see.

Help them remember why they said "yes."

And give them the strength to keep saying it every day after.

In Jesus' name,

Amen.

Chapter Three
Blessings

Rightly Wed & Groomed

If *"Bliss"* was the melody and *"Blisters"* the dissonance, then *"Blessings"* is surely the rich harmony—notes of mercy, grace, and laughter blending into a song only time and tenacity could compose. This is the chapter of survival, of renewal, of being kept when we could have fallen apart. It is the chapter of *"still."*

We are still together.

Still in love.

Still growing.

Still walking the path God laid before us—sometimes limping, yes, but never losing faith.

There's something beautiful about waking up beside the same woman for over three decades. Her hair may be getting streaks of silver now, and my knees a little more rebellious, but the sound of her laughter is still the music of my mornings. And her presence, even in silence, still feels like home.

After all the early turbulence—my failings, our struggles, her tears, my silence—something extraordinary happened: we matured. Not overnight, not without friction, but with God's steady hand at the wheel, we became not just husband and wife, but partners in life and purpose. I'd asked God for the love to return—and return it did, deeper and more rooted than before. He took what was fading and made it flourish.

Our home slowly became a haven. We celebrated each birthday, ours and our children's, even the foster girls—three of them—each with their own spark and stories. Our house became a classroom, a church pew, a sanctuary, and sometimes, yes, a battlefield (especially when the last slice of cake or piece of chicken went missing). But more than anything, it became a place of love.

We were still working to complete our first home—walls that knew our prayers, witnessed our reconciliations, and echoed with the giggles of children. And still we were not maximising the use of the car. Ah, plans I had! But romantic drives, weekend escapes, a creek picnic here or there were rare, but lots of time I found myself driving home with the best intentions...only to park and find my couch more persuasive than a promenade. Shelly, ever the eager explorer, would nudge, hint, and then finally declare, *"You don't feel the same about me like you used to!"* And I'd grumble, scratch my head, and say, *"It's not the feelings that's gone, my love—it's just hiding behind a long day."*

She never let me settle. Not in life, not in love, and certainly not in faith.

As I continued serving as Assistant Pastor Shelly stood by me—not just beside me in the pews, but behind me in prayer and ahead of me in encouragement. She wore many hats: Sunday School leader, teacher, mother, chef, counsellor, prayer warrior, and unofficial family comedian. She loved children like they were born of her own heart and carried herself with grace—even when carrying more burdens than most knew.

I still remember 2005, the rupture in our rhythm. Cerebral aneurysm. Unconscious for weeks. Time, suddenly, slowed to a crawl. I still remember riding that elevator down from Mt. Hope Hospital, feeling like each level brought me closer to grief. Tears—not dramatic, just steady—rolled down my cheek. For the first time then, I tasted the terrifying thought of life without her.

But God.

Two words that have saved many stories.

She lived. Not just survived, but returned to herself—to us. That was no ordinary blessing. That was mercy walking into the hospital room, brushing the veil of death aside and saying, *"Not yet."*

Years later, another blow—breast cancer in 2024. And once again, I watched her stand tall. We both have our physical battles now, our aches and pills and doctor's appointments. But we walk together, leaning on each other, and more importantly, leaning on God.

She still smiles. Still laughs. Sometimes still nags (to keep me sharp, she says). But she also still prays, still serves, still lights up the room with her gentle strength.

I've learned that blessings don't always look like new things—they often look like old things that didn't give up. A marriage that withstood. A faith that endured. A woman who stayed. A man who grew. A God who never let go.

As I now serve as Senior Pastor, I don't preach about perfect homes—I preach about healed ones. I don't boast about flawless love—I boast about grace. Because if our story says anything, it says this:

God is faithful.

And marriage—when rightly wed and groomed—is not just a legal contract or cultural expectation. It's a covenant. One that requires both husband and wife to be groomed— pruned by experience, refined by Scripture, softened by forgiveness, and strengthened by service.

Reflections & Prayers

Husbands, love your wives, even as Christ also
loved the church, and gave himself for it.

– Ephesians 5:25

This verse reminds me that my love for Shelly must be sacrificial. It's not about being right, or being served, but about serving—even when tired, even when misunderstood. Lord, help me to love like You love.

Though one may be overpowered, two can
defend themselves. A cord of three strands is
not quickly broken.

—Ecclesiastes 4:12

That third strand—God—is why we are still standing. Through every storm, His presence was the anchor.

A Husband's Prayer

Father,

Thank You for the woman You gave me. Thank You for every laugh, every lesson, every lingering moment. Help me to cherish her always—to see her not only as my wife, but as Your daughter, entrusted to my care.

Let our marriage reflect Your heart, and may our story point others to You.

Amen.

A Wife's Prayer (on behalf of Shelly)

Lord,

Thank You for my husband. Thank You for bringing us through fire and flood. Give me strength on the hard days, laughter on the light ones, and grace for the in-between. May our home be filled with peace and purpose.

Amen.

So here we are—thirty-seven years in. The man once known as *"Spere"* is now just *"Honey"* or *"Pastor."* And the woman once admired from afar is now my anchor, my answer to prayer, my blessing.

And if you ask me the secret?

It's not in the champagne, or dining, or coordinated outfits (though Shelly did love those).

It's in commitment. It's in Christ.

It's in being Rightly Wed & Groomed.

Chapter Four
Foundations of Forever

Building on Solid Rock

Marriage, like a house, is only as strong as what it's built on. Some begin with passion, some with good intentions, but only those grounded in faith and truth can endure the test of time.

After years of being together, Shelly and I learned that the foundation of a good marriage isn't just romance — it's righteousness. The butterflies fade, but what takes their place is something even more beautiful: security, trust, and peace.

When we were younger, I thought that love alone could fix anything. But over time, I realised love must have something to stand on. If you build your marriage on emotions, it will crumble under pressure. If you build it on money, it will shake when the economy turns. But when you build it on Christ, it will stand through any storm.

"Except the Lord build the house, they labour in vain that build it."

— Psalm 127:1 (KJV)

We had our share of storms. There were days when silence filled the space that laughter used to occupy. There were misunderstandings that didn't make sense to either of us, and times when we questioned if we were even hearing each other at all. But every time, God reminded us that this marriage was not ours to quit — it was His to sustain.

We learned that reconciliation is not weakness; it is wisdom. The longer you live together, the more you understand that winning an argument often means losing peace. But choosing peace — even when pride tells you otherwise — is the truest form of strength.

Shelly had a way of reminding me of that. She would say, *"You can't talk peace and walk pride, Walter."* And she was right. Peace in marriage often begins with one person deciding to bend — not because they are wrong, but because they value the relationship more than the quarrel.

Over the years, we began to develop habits that kept our home steady:

We prayed before reacting.

We laughed more often than we complained.

We gave thanks for small things — a shared meal, a quiet morning, a safe return home.

And even when we failed at those things, we kept trying.

Because that's what marriage really is — two imperfect people refusing to give up on each other.

"Therefore, everyone who hears these words of mine and puts them into practice is like a wise man who built his house on the rock."

— Matthew 7:24 (NIV)

Our rock was not always visible to others, but it was firm beneath us. There were days when my faith carried Shelly, and days when her faith carried me. When one grew weary, the other interceded. And somehow, that rhythm of grace kept us standing.

If you are married — or hope to be — make sure your foundation is not made of convenience or compatibility alone. Build it on covenant. Covenants don't collapse when the weather changes. They endure because they are rooted in divine purpose.

A wise builder knows that even the strongest walls will crack if the base shifts. So, every now and then, take time to inspect your foundation. Ask God to show you where it needs repair — and then rebuild together, brick by brick, with patience and prayer.

Reflection & Devotion – Building on Christ

Every couple dreams of a perfect home, but no home is perfect until the Master Builder is invited to stay. Christ is not just a visitor in marriage — He must be the cornerstone.

> *"For no one can lay any foundation other than the one already laid, which is Jesus Christ."*
>
> — *1 Corinthians 3:11 (NIV)*

If you've been shaken, don't give up. A cracked wall doesn't mean the house is doomed — it just means the foundation needs reinforcing. Invite God back into the centre. Rebuild with forgiveness, cement it with love, and let the Word of God be your blueprint.

Prayer

Lord, thank You for being the solid rock beneath our feet. Teach us to build our marriages on You — not on feelings, wealth, or convenience, but on Your truth. When the rains come and the winds blow, may our love stand firm.

Strengthen every couple reading this, and remind them that a house built with You will never fall.

In Jesus' name, Amen.

Chapter Five
Faith in the Fire

There comes a point in every marriage when the honeymoon laughter fades and real life begin its testing. It is not that the love is gone, but that it begins to take on a new form — one that must be fuelled by commitment, patience, and prayer.

For Shelly and me, that season came quietly, without warning. There were days when joy flowed freely and nights when silence spoke louder than words. But through it all, faith became our anchor.

I have learned that love, even in Christian marriages, does not grow stronger by accident. It matures through moments that bruise the ego, test your faith, and call for forgiveness even when you feel justified to do otherwise.

There were times I had to kneel beside my bed, asking God to help me love again the way I once did. Marriage had a way of exposing my pride — that subtle enemy that whispers, *"You are right and she is wrong."* But God, in His gentle wisdom, taught me that being right does not build a marriage — being humble does.

"Likewise, ye husbands, dwell with them according to knowledge, giving honour unto the wife, as unto the weaker vessel, and as being heirs together of the grace of life; that your prayers be not hindered."

— 1 Peter 3:7 (KJV)

There were moments when I felt like giving up — not walking out, but emotionally shutting down. And yet, each time I thought the flame would die, something happened: a word from God, a smile from Shelly, a quiet conviction that we had come too far to turn back.

It is strange how love can be both fragile and fierce. Fragile, because careless words can wound it deeply. Fierce, because real love fights to survive the storm.

I watched Shelly grow into the kind of woman who reflected both grace and grit. Her laughter, even in difficult seasons, reminded me of God's faithfulness. Sometimes, she would say something that sounded simple but carried weight, like, *"We can't keep fighting if we're on the same side."* That line has saved us more than once.

We began learning that marriage wasn't about winning arguments but about winning together. Prayer replaced pride; forgiveness replaced fault-finding. We still stumbled, but now we stumbled forward — together.

"A threefold cord is not quickly broken."

— Ecclesiastes 4:12 (KJV)

The more I yielded to God's Word; the more peace returned to our home. The more I led in love rather than demand, the more respect naturally followed. We discovered that every time we invited God into the middle of our conflict, He brought calm where there was chaos.

Through all of this, one truth became clear: faith is not just for the church — it is for the home. It keeps you grounded when emotions rise, steady when disappointment hits, and hopeful when tomorrow looks uncertain.

When fire comes — and it will — let it refine you, not consume you. Because when faith walks hand in hand with love, no flame can destroy what God has joined together.

Reflection & Devotion: Love Refined by Fire

Marriage is like gold — its beauty is revealed through refining. The seasons of testing are not designed to destroy us but to draw us closer to God and to each other. When the fire gets hot, remember: God is still in the midst of it.

"When you walk through the fire, you shall not be burned; The flames shall not set you ablaze."

— Isaiah 43:2 (NIV)

Let prayer be your oxygen when love feels faint. Let forgiveness be your language when tempers flare. Let faith be your anchor when life's storms blow strong.

Prayer

Heavenly Father,

Thank You for the gift of marriage — for the joy it brings and for the lessons it teaches. When the heat of life's trials threatens to overwhelm us, help us to remember that You are the refiner and not the destroyer. Strengthen our love, deepen our patience, and keep our hearts bound together in grace.

May our homes be places where Your peace abides and Your presence is felt. In Jesus' name,

Amen.

Chapter Six
Moulded and Held

Marriage, as we were slowly discovering, was not just about having a good time or even making it through the bad ones—it was about being shaped. Moulded. Refined. Not unlike clay in the hands of a Master Potter. Only, in our case, the clay came with opinions, emotions, preferences, and a strong will.

Shelly and I came from two very different households. Her upbringing was deeply communal, filled with people and noise and unfiltered expressions of love and discipline. Mine was quieter, structured in a different way. These differences weren't always obvious while we were dating, but as the days of marriage began to stretch into months and years, they made their presence known.

Take, for instance, how we managed conflict. Shelly was immediate— *"let's sort this now."* She could follow you from the kitchen to the veranda with the unfinished part of an argument. I, on the other hand, believed in the ministry of silence—go quiet, pray, and let time soften things. Needless to say, the early years saw a few frustrating stand-offs that could have made a good sitcom episode.

We had to learn a lot—and quickly. I had to learn that my silence, though peaceful to me, could feel like abandonment to her. She had to learn that words, though healing to her, could sometimes cut when wielded in haste. Somewhere between her passion and my restraint, we had to find our own rhythm. And thank God, we did.

Financial stretching was another chapter in the *"moulding"* manual. There were days when we had to stretch the dollar to make ends meet, but we thank God we were always able to flavour a pot that served six or seven meals. The days when toothpaste had to be coaxed out like it was a stingy relative. Yet, even in that, we laughed. We joked. We prayed. We built memories.

One particularly memorable moment came when I was trying to fix a pipe under the kitchen sink. Armed with confidence and very little plumbing knowledge, I launched into the task while Shelly stood nearby, "supervising." Ten minutes later, she was soaked, I was laughing, and we both realised that maybe calling the plumber wouldn't have hurt. Now, I would handle that job like a *"pro"* and garner much praise from her.

So, we were learning. About compromise. About listening. About holding each other's hands, even when we didn't fully agree, we learnt that love was not just a feeling—it was a decision. A choice to keep walking together, even when the road curved sharply or was littered with the unexpected.

And while we were being moulded, we were also being held. Held by the grace of God. Held by the wisdom of those ahead of us who shared their stories. Held by the community around us who prayed and laughed and sometimes wept with us.

Reflection & Devotional Moment

"But we have this treasure in jars of clay to show that this all-surpassing power is from God and not from us."

—2 Corinthians 4:7 (NIV)

Thought

Marriage is one of the places God uses to shape us into who we were meant to be—not just for each other, but for His purpose. And in that shaping, we are never left alone.

Prayer

Father,

Thank You for the beauty of transformation within marriage. For every challenge that teaches us grace, and every moment that binds us closer. Keep shaping us, keep holding us. Let us never forget that even when it's hard, You are present—moulding with love and purpose.

Amen.

Chapter Seven
Blessed in Battle

Every marriage goes through seasons—sunshine and shadow, blossoms and bruises. By this time in our journey, Shelly and I had experienced enough of both to recognise a pattern: when trials came, blessings were not far behind.

It would be dishonest to say we never had moments when the weight felt too heavy—when ministry pressures, parenting struggles, financial burdens, or simply our own humanity came crashing through our front door. But what made those moments survivable, even sacred, was how God met us in the middle of the battle.

I remember once, we had what I like to call *a "Holy Ghost argument."* You know the kind—words were exchanged, the air got a little tense, and both of us felt misunderstood. Yet somewhere in the middle of that disagreement, I found myself praying out loud. It wasn't even a deeply spiritual moment—it was a desperate one. But the presence of God filled the room, and suddenly the argument lost its edge. What remained was the softness that only grace can bring.

Parenting was another battlefield that turned into a blessing. Raising our children was a joy, yes, but also a constant classroom. There were late nights, hospital visits, prayer vigils over school grades and choices, especially some made by our son in high school. There were questions at times when we couldn't answer right away. There were victories too—graduations, spiritual milestones, *"thank-you-Daddy"* and *"I-love-you-Mummy"* moments that made us want to tear up at times. We didn't get everything right. But we stayed together. And somehow, that made us stronger than the sum of our mistakes.

The Ministry brought its share of trials. Serving others while walking through our own valleys sometimes felt unfair. There were days when we ministered healing while our own hearts were bleeding. But it was in those moments of spiritual fatigue that we truly understood what it meant to be *"blessed in battle."* God's strength never failed to meet us.

I often say: Marriage is not a shield from war—it is your frontline companion. Shelly and I had to fight together—not against each other. And once we got that right, battles became less bitter and far more bonding. We became warriors in the same uniform.

There were moments we would just sit quietly, her head on my shoulder, no words spoken, just a silent agreement that we're still here. Still fighting. Still loving. Still believing that what God joined, no man, no trial, no season would pull apart.

And then came the blessings—sometimes financial breakthroughs, sometimes open doors we had prayed long for, sometimes just the peace of going to bed with nothing left unresolved. We learnt not to measure blessings by the size of a miracle, but by the nearness of God.

Yes, the battles were real. But so were the blessings. And many of those blessings wore the face of my wife, the sound of my children's laughter, or the peace that flooded our home after a storm.

Reflection & Devotional Moment

"The Lord will fight for you; you need only to be still."

—Exodus 14:14 (NIV)

Thought

Marriage will test your faith, your patience, and your strength. But it will also deepen your trust, refine your character, and bring unexpected joy. The presence of battles does not cancel the presence of blessings—they often share the same space.

Prayer

Lord,

Thank You for the blessings hidden inside battles. Teach us to lean on each other, to fight for—not against—our spouse. Strengthen our hearts and remind us that You are always present, even in the fire.

Amen.

Chapter Eight
Still Growing, Still Together

The seasons of marriage do not come with announcements. They arrive quietly—sometimes in the laughter of grandsons echoing down the hallway, other times in the sound of a grown child closing the door behind them, with burdens too heavy for parents to lift.

We never imagined that after decades of raising our children, we would once again find ourselves in a home where bedrooms were filled, shoes lined the doorway, and toys reappeared in the living room. Today, we still have two of our adult children living with us, and two grandsons who've brought joy, noise, and a new rhythm to our lives.

But this chapter has not come without its challenges.

It broke our hearts when our daughter's marriage fell apart. We had prayed, supported, and hoped, but in the end, it did not last. Seeing your child grieve a dream you once shared with them is one of the quietest kinds of pain. And yet, in her brokenness, she and her sons returned home—a place that will always be open to them.

Living with adult children, especially in a full house, has tested our patience and our partnership. It sometimes feels like we are balancing the dynamics of four separate households under one roof. And then there's the age-old trap: it seems to them that I favour our daughter, while to me, Shelly appears to favour our son. We laugh about it later, but in the heat of the moment, it can be a real flame-stoker.

The tension often arises over simple things—chores undone, misunderstandings, responsibilities unmet. Voices rise. Tempers flare. And there are days when side-taking is as subtle as silence, or as loud as storming off. But here's the part that matters: we don't stay there. We have learnt to return, to talk, to laugh, to pray.

I promised myself long ago that I would love Shelly the Bible way. Not only when she checks every box, but especially when she doesn't. Not only when she is her sweetest self, but also when she is tired, annoyed, or distracted. I cannot speak for what she has promised herself—but I know that she chooses me daily, and that counts for more than words.

We are still learning how to parent grown children. Still learning how to grandparent with grace. Still learning how to love through shifting roles and emotional minefields. But we're learning together. And that's the difference.

Devotional Reflection: The Love That Stays

"Love is patient, love is kind... It keeps no record of wrongs. Love never fails."

—1 Corinthians 13:4–8 (NIV)

When Paul described love in his letter to the Corinthians, he wasn't writing about courtship or honeymoon sweetness. He was writing about covenant. The love that stays, works, forgives, grows, and outlasts the tough days.

To love *"the Bible way"* is to forgive quickly, to serve even when tired, and to remember that your spouse is not your opponent. They are your covenant partner—even when the battle is not outside but inside your own home.

Prayer

Father,

Thank You for teaching us to love beyond comfort. Help us to parent wisely, to grandparent graciously, and to cherish each other even in the testing ground of shared life. May our home be a place of healing, not just for us, but for the generations coming after.

Amen.

Chapter Nine
Reignited and Rooted

Marriage has truly been an adventure. Ours has been a journey of fun, thrills, excitement, hearty laughter, and yes—boisterous storms too. We've climbed mountains together, trudged through valleys, and sometimes wandered across unfamiliar terrains that seemed unnavigable. But through every twist and turn, we stuck it out—through the thick and thin, the highs and the lows. And by God's grace, we're still here, stronger, wiser, and deeper in love than we were when we started.

Every mountain we climbed gave us courage for the next. Every valley taught us humility and dependence on God. We learned from both the sunshine and the rain. Sometimes we danced, sometimes we stumbled, but we never stopped moving forward. I made the Word of God my counsel, and I say without shame: if I hadn't, I might have thrown in the towel more than once.

I don't want to sound superhuman—Pastors are people too. I've had moments when frustration threatened to get the better of me. Times when I vented to a close confidant just to stay sane. I didn't always have the answer, and I wasn't always eager to do the right thing—maybe it was pride, or just plain weariness. But I made a vow to love Shelly the Bible way: not based on conditions, but out of conviction. It's not always easy, but it's always worth it.

And here we are. Many years in, as I stated earlier, our children are grown, some living with us again. Life has cycled us back to a busy household with two adult children and two grandboys. The home is loud, lively, and sometimes lopsided when it comes to who does certain chores. Yes, Chores become battlegrounds, tensions rise, and tempers flare—but not for long. We bounce back. We always bounce back. Because bitterness has no place in a covenant, and love is still our foundation.

We've been through enough to counsel others now. And what a joy it is to sit with couples—young and older—and share what God has taught us. Marriage and family mean so much to me that I feel a call beyond just our congregation. The world needs strong homes. The world needs living proof that it can still work.

Rightly Wed and Groomed isn't just a book title. It's the heart of a movement. A few years ago, I launched a special event under that same name—a vow renewal celebration for married couples, in collaboration between Fruits of Calvary Assembly and Praise Tabernacle churches. It was unforgettable: sixty couples, dressed in their best, redeclaring their love. The day began with a joyous photo shoot and continued with a motorcade, complete with police escort and sirens wailing through the streets of Linden—Wismar and Mackenzie alike. Curiosity peaked as onlookers watched a parade of love roll by.

We gathered before Bishop R. Mertland Messiah to renew our vows. Then came the gala dinner, the toasts, the cutting of the cake, the romantic kiss, the dancing—it was a celebration of love and legacy. Reignite the Fire – Fan the Flame, we called it. And I'm pleased to say Part Two is being planned for 2025.

This book is part of that flame. A continuation of the passion to share, to bless, and to inspire.

I must thank our church family, who each year celebrate our wedding anniversary in grand style—complete with cake, sparkling drinks, gifts, and loving tributes. These acts of love fuel our journey and remind us we're not in this alone.

And yes, I have my moments in church where I challenge couples to keep the romance alive—hug your spouse, hold hands, look them in the eyes, remind each other of your love. You'd be surprised how awkward that can be for some—but oh, how beautiful when they obey.

Even now, writing these lines, I feel that old fire bubbling up in my chest. It's 11:07 PM, Shelly is snoring softly beside me, one arm draped over me. And yes, there's a grandson snuggled in too, which may not be romantic, but it is real—and I wouldn't trade it for the world.

I'm grateful I didn't give up after those first two rough years. Had I walked away then, we wouldn't have this story to tell.

Reflection & Devotion: Reignited and Rooted.

Theme: The Long Game of Love

Scripture: "Love bears all things, believes all things, hopes all things, endures all things. Love never fails."

— 1 Corinthians 13:7-8 (NKJV)

Reflection

The journey of marriage is not a sprint; it is a long-distance marathon. Along the way, you'll face potholes and detours—moments that test your resolve and tug at your commitment. But as this chapter reminds us, staying the course yields fruit that no short-lived romance can replicate.

Enduring love is forged in the furnace of life's pressures. Every trial becomes a testimony, every tear a tender memory. What keeps a marriage anchored is not always the absence of conflict, but the presence of grace and the practice of forgiveness.

Even the smallest shared joy—a quiet moment at bedtime, a hand-held during prayer, or a look exchanged across a room—can rekindle what seemed to fade. Love, when rooted in God and nurtured with intention, will grow stronger with time.

Devotional Thought

Take a moment to thank God for the journey you've walked with your spouse. Whether it's been one year or many decades, each season carries lessons and blessings. Reflect on a storm you've weathered together, and consider what God taught you through it. Then, thank Him for the strength to endure and the grace to love still.

Prayer

Heavenly Father,

Thank You for walking with us through the winding path of marriage. Thank You for grace that forgives, for joy that renews, and for love that never fails. Teach us to honour one another, to lean on You, and to keep the fire of our covenant alive. May our marriage be a testimony of Your faithfulness, and may it be a blessing to others.

In Jesus' name,

Amen.

Chapter Ten
Bonded for Life

The concept of being bound together in marriage is described in the most awe-inspiring language—words that evoke both wonder and challenge. *"The two shall become one flesh." "What God has joined together, let no man separate."* These phrases sound majestic and reassuring, especially to couples who are rightly wed and groomed. But while being "rightly wed" is one thing, the grooming process is where the real test lies. It is often in this phase that the troubles emerge, and the way a couple navigates those moments determines the strength of the bond that holds them together. No inferior glue—no cheap imitation of love—will withstand the pressures of life.

As the saying goes: You may fall in love at first sight, but marriage is an eye-opener.

Shelly and I have lived this truth. We've walked the talk, and still the journey isn't over. We've conquered giants together—not in our own strength, but through our reliance on God. When we are united, we're a force to reckon with. Greater is He who is in us than he who is in the world. But when we turn against each other, we become no match for the enemy. That's just the honest truth.

Thirty-seven years together is not thirty-seven days, or even months—it's over 324,000 hours. That's a lot of time. Our love has had to endure, and it has. It has flowed from a blissful, magical spring, surged over mountaintops, then tumbled into valleys. Sometimes it has raged like rapids—violent, panicked, breathless—and yet it has always found a way to soar again, to sparkle in the sunshine on the next peak.

We've learned that if it's going to be good, we have to make it good. Nothing can be taken for granted. For example, compliments work wonders for Shelly. If I say I like a particular meal, I better mean it—because it's going to be repeated often! That's a trait she picked up from her mother. While she appreciates gifts, money brings her a special kind of energy. She also loves outings and fun times more than I do, and I'm learning to meet her there—because that's what love does.

Now, she can deliver some top-tier sarcasm when she's not getting her way, but I've developed a kind of immunity over the years—not in a way that shuts her out, but one that keeps the peace and protects our bond. I deal with her according to knowledge. That principle has been vital in our growth. We've learned that knowing what brings joy to your spouse, and intentionally doing it, is what keeps the journey exciting. Likewise, avoiding the things that cause injury—emotional or otherwise—is just as important.

I've never called my wife insulting names. But yes, I've done things that caused emotional pain, and I regret those moments. I've discovered that "sorry" is a good word, and meaning it is a good attitude. If you find it hard to say sorry, then do your best to avoid offending in the first place.

Our love has been tried and tested, and while we are highly qualified by experience, we're not masters of the art—not yet. But I believe our lessons can help others, especially those whose marriages have become emotionally or spiritually impoverished. Someone once joked, *"Marriage is like a walk in the park—Jurassic Park."* That's the reality for many couples. But even in the chaos, healing is possible.

You are the stars of your story, and the directors, too. You get to shape the script from where you stand. If you're still together, despite what has happened, that in itself is a blessing. You can start over. Plan a weekend getaway. Do something romantic. Laugh again. Laugh about the silly things that once got in your way. And above all—pray.

Prayer changed everything for us. I said earlier that, after two years, I thought I had lost my love for Shelly. But through prayer, God restored it. That was thirty-five years ago. If we're granted another thirty-five, we'll be grandmasters in this thing called love.

Marriage, in its truest form, is beautiful. But it only works when God is in it. If He's not, the enemy will surely find room to destroy it. God's design is restorative and redemptive. Whatever is broken, He can mend. Whatever is good, He can make better.

So, whether it's Shelly, Shelburn, or Mendeth...or Spere, Pastor, or Wallie—we belong to each other. We have a love that's meant to last forever.

Babes, I love you.

Reflection & Devotion

"Therefore what God has joined together, let no one separate."

— Mark 10:9 (NIV)

Reflect

Marriage is not simply a contract—it is a divine covenant, forged by God and intended to be unbreakable. Yet, every covenant must endure seasons of testing. In Chapter Ten, we explored the metaphor of glue: cheap adhesives cannot hold under pressure. The truth is, neither can cheap commitments. Marital love must be made of something stronger—grace, truth, patience, forgiveness, and above all, a shared devotion to God.

Ask yourself

What kind of glue is holding your marriage together?

Is it duty?

Habit? Social pressure?

Or is it the grace of God and a daily decision to love?

Devotional Thought

Love may begin with a spark, but it's kept alive with fuel—intentionality, affection, and divine help. One of the greatest gifts you can give your spouse is the assurance that even in the worst of times, you're still choosing them.

Marriage doesn't thrive on perfection; it thrives on persistence. The ability to say *"I'm sorry"* and mean it. The maturity to love your spouse where they are, while growing together into who God wants you both to become.

Just like Shelly and I, you may walk through "Jurassic Park" moments. But if God is at the centre, your love can survive anything—even giants.

Prayer

Lord, thank You for the gift of covenant love. Help me to love with intention and forgive with grace. Strengthen the bond in my marriage, not with cheap promises, but with the strong glue of Your presence, patience, and power. Where we've wounded each other, bring healing. Where we've drifted, draw us closer. Let our love be a testimony of Your faithfulness. In Jesus' name, amen.

Action Point

Write your spouse a short note expressing something you genuinely appreciate about them. Then, schedule a moment this week—whether a walk, champagne, or a meal—just to connect or reconnect without distractions. Let love breathe again.

Chapter Eleven
Another Chapter

With Rightly Wed & Groomed approaching on October 18 and our tickets already purchased for London — a two-week trip we had long looked forward to — I began to feel uneasy about how everything would work out. After three days, Shelly was discharged from the hospital, though she still wasn't one hundred percent.

Our children were deeply concerned and advised us not to travel under the circumstances. I wanted to be that good husband who would do it for her sake, and I suspected she wanted to be that loving daughter who would do it for her mother. In fact, Shelly would often bend over backwards for her. So, to London we were heading.

By now, you would have discovered that London is one of my favourite places, but something within me kept whispering, "This is not the time." Yet I ignored that gentle nudge.

We left Guyana on September 15 for the UK, and our journey was smooth — without any major incident, except for Shelly's intermittent coughing, just enough to raise concern. By the time we arrived in London, the coughing had worsened. She was exhaling in groans, and immediately, I knew this was not going to be good for our holiday. Still, I hoped for the best — for her, and for us.

Ten days were spent in London — ten days that turned out to be the most agonising we had ever spent there. Shelly could hardly hold a long conversation. Whenever she tried to speak, she would start coughing uncontrollably. You can imagine what that can do to a vacation, long or short. She eventually lost her appetite to the point where I literally had to feed her at times just to get her to eat a little. Nights were another ordeal — restless, painful, filled with whispered prayers and broken sleep.

Yet, through prayer, we made it through each night. Fortunately, our stay was shorter than our usual four-week vacations. The shopping sprees that we usually enjoyed together were reduced to three brief outings. Even then, the third had to be cut short as I saw her groaning in discomfort. So, there were no dining outs, no sightseeing as we were accustomed to — only endurance and faith.

Efforts to get medical attention while in the UK bore no real fruit, but God was faithful until the very last night of our trip.

September 25 — the day of our return to Guyana — came as a relief. We rose early that morning to prepare for our 7:00 a.m. check-in at Gatwick Airport, an hour's drive from where we were staying. We had packed everything the night before, with help from her mother, Joycelyn, and cousin Roxanne, both of whom were visibly concerned about Shelly's condition and had come to see her off.

That Thursday morning, my wife mustered every ounce of strength she had to get herself ready. Watching her was painful. I had brought along a pack of ginger sweets from Guyana, barely used, which she had occasionally requested during her coughing spells. I also had a few small containers of gum we had purchased in London.

The taxi arrived, and after exchanging hugs with her mum and cousin, we left. From the time we boarded, the ride was almost nightmarish. The coughing grew worse — relentless and draining. The taxi driver became concerned, asking more than once, *"Are you okay, miss?"* My only recourse was to keep passing her ginger sweets and gum at her frequent requests. I thank the Lord I had them in abundance — they became her "medication" for the next twelve hours until we reached Guyana.

When we arrived at the airport, the driver was gracious enough to handle our luggage and ensure we were checked in before departing. His kindness meant much, especially since I too was dealing with my own physical challenges and had requested wheelchair assistance — which ended up being given to Shelly.

Our three-hour wait in the lounge felt like torture, especially for me. She was not eating, growing weaker by the minute. I remember her softly saying, *"Call our son in Guyana and ask him to pray for me."* I was confused at first, since I was right there beside her — but that was one of those moments when faith and fear wrestled inside me.

Sometimes, the twists and turns of life and marriage come so suddenly that we feel utterly unprepared — and that was exactly how I felt. Yet even there, God gave strength for both of us.

A brief light moment came when one of two ladies seated next to us noticed Shelly's fingernails and remarked, *"How lovely they are!"* Shelly smiled, and the other lady agreed. Proudly, I told them, *"They were done by my daughter."* For a moment, her smile returned, and so did a little joy.

Flight time came, and we boarded — beginning what would be one of the most intense journeys of our lifetime. We were heading home, but with a *"devil"* in my wife's chest. We had no confirmed medical report beyond what we knew before leaving Guyana — that she had recently recovered from a lung infection and a small buildup of fluid.

Having completed chemotherapy only weeks before, we suspected that whatever was happening was related to her ongoing battle with cancer. But there was no way to confirm. So, there we were — thousands of feet in the air, armed with gum, ginger sweets, bottled water, and prayer.

The flight was scheduled to stop in St. Lucia before heading to Guyana. That first leg felt like a spiritual marathon. I prayed every kind of prayer I knew, sensing the urgency of every breath she took. Each time she reached for a sweet or whispered *"pray,"* my heart would clench with both fear and faith.

Breathing grew more laboured at times, but we tried not to alert the airline staff, fearing they might remove us from the flight to avoid any responsibility. So, we prayed quietly, trusting God to see us through.

At one point, she turned to me and said anxiously, *"Call up the intercessors to pray."* Seeing my puzzled look, she clarified, *"I mean — call them up in the spirit."* That moment touched me deeply. Her faith, even in weakness, was fierce.

After nearly eight turbulent hours that only we could truly describe, the plane landed in St. Lucia. Being on the ground brought some relief. Passengers disembarked, others boarded, and soon we were airborne again — another stretch of faith and endurance.

Even as I write this, I feel the ache of that journey. I only wanted to be by my wife's side for that short ten-day trip — something we had done so often, since she never liked to travel without me. Her mother, Joycelyn, felt the same way — believing that husband and wife should always travel together.

The previous year, Shelly had travelled alone to the USA and then London, while I stayed behind. I never pursued a US visa — didn't feel led to — so I couldn't accompany her then. But this time, I was glad beyond words that I was with her.

I reassured her that we would make it home. *"We've done the long leg,"* I told her. *"We can handle the short one."* That seemed to give her hope. I sang softly for her, worshipping as we flew, creating a gentle, prayerful atmosphere around us. I encouraged her with Scripture, and before long, the pilot's voice came over the intercom: *"Ladies and gentlemen, we will be landing in twenty minutes."*

Relief swept over me — but a new and more painful chapter was about to begin.

As we disembarked, Shelly could barely stand. We quickly secured a wheelchair and cleared immigration. Our son was waiting outside; his face filled with both joy and worry. With his help, we got Shelly into the car and began the familiar drive home to Linden.

But it was yet another difficult ride. Her breathing grew more laboured with each passing mile. We phoned one of her doctors, Dr. Isaacs, explaining the situation. Without hesitation, she alerted the emergency ward at the Linden Hospital Complex — the same hospital where Shelly worked.

When we arrived, everything was already in place. X-rays were done immediately, and the results showed one lung almost completely filled with fluid. The revelation was heartbreaking. Still, I thanked God, she had made it that far — and was still alive.

While at A&E, the medical team began draining the fluid from her lungs — almost two litres in total. That news hit me like a powerful blow to the stomach. To think that my wife had travelled those long journeys across the sky like a drowning woman—it broke my heart.

After the fluid was drawn, Shelly was admitted to the ICU. I was completely unprepared for what lay ahead, but I was willing and ready to do all I could to see my wife get better and return to her normal self again.

While in ICU, her condition worsened. The fluid began building up rapidly again. Her doctor grew concerned and consulted with the family about performing a thoracentesis — a painful but necessary procedure to remove the fluid. We had no other option but to agree.

Being the strong woman she was, Shelly pulled through it bravely. More fluid was removed, and after four days in ICU she was transferred to the city's hospital for further testing and treatment.

It's worth noting that since arriving from the UK, she had not yet reached our home in Linden. Now she was being transported from one hospital to another, still unwell and unable to rest in her own bed.

But God, in His mercy, surrounded us with help. I thank Him for the strong support team He placed around me — our son, our daughter, and our foster daughter, Sammilyn. We *"banded our bellies,"* as we say in Guyana, and made every sacrifice possible. We were determined to see Shelly get well. Her faith told her she could, and we all hung onto that faith with her.

Then came the report from Georgetown Hospital. The doctors' findings were not what we wanted to hear. It felt as though someone had sucked the very air from my lungs. The cancer had spread to both lungs, and there was a mass on one that would likely affect her breathing from time to time. It was devastating news.

Shelly spent another six days at Georgetown Public Hospital before being discharged. She was told she would need to remain on oxygen until her collapsed lungs could recover. That brought a new challenge: ensuring she had a constant oxygen supply at home.

But once again, God made provision. Through the overwhelming generosity of her colleagues at the Linden Hospital Complex, as well as our family, friends, and church community, everything she needed for home care was supplied. The prayers of God's people — near and far — rose continually on our behalf, and we were deeply grateful.

Reflection & Inspiration: Faith in the Fire

It is one thing to preach about faith; it is another to live it out when your heart is breaking and your strength feels gone. I have stood by hospital beds before, prayed for others, and comforted those in distress. But standing beside my wife — my life partner — watching her battle for every breath, tested me in ways I could never have imagined.

Yet, even in that valley, I discovered something sacred: God was there. Not in the noise, but in the stillness. Not only in the healing, but in the holding.

"When you pass through the waters, I will be with you; and through the rivers, they shall not overflow you: When you walk through the fire, you shall not be burned."

— Isaiah 43:2 (KJV)

Faith does not mean we are exempt from suffering; it means we are accompanied through it.

In those long days and nights, I saw what true love looks like — not the glitter of wedding days, but the grit of shared pain. The vows we made decades ago took on new meaning: *"for better or worse, in sickness and in health."*

Love, when refined by suffering, becomes unbreakable.

Faith, when tested by fire, becomes unshakable.

As we cared for Shelly and trusted God each day, I realised something profound: miracles don't always come in the form of instant healing — sometimes the miracle is in the strength to endure, the grace to smile, and the peace to keep believing.

"My grace is sufficient for thee: for my strength is made perfect in weakness."

— *2 Corinthians 12:9 (KJV)*

So, if your marriage is walking through a dark valley — hold hands tighter.

Pray longer.

Love deeper.

Even when healing seems delayed, hope is still alive.

The Final Chapter
Till Death

When I set out to write this book, it was to share the story of our marriage — between Shelly and me. At that time, we were in our thirty-sixth year of marriage. I felt a deep passion to share our journey — the highs, the lows, and all the places in between. That's how the title Rightly Wed and Groomed: Bliss, Blisters, Blessings was born. It was also the name of the signature wedded event I had hosted for married couples, and it seemed fitting to carry that same theme into a book.

I wanted to help inspire husbands and wives to make the best of their marriage and live out their best lives for each other. Too many marriages are struggling; too many have hit rock bottom, seemingly beyond repair. From creation, marriage and the family have been under constant attack — and that attack has only intensified. But it was never God's plan for marriages to be bitter, battered, or broken. That came through sin.

This book was meant to be a surprise — a tribute to Shelly, my beloved wife, for the many years we shared together. I never thought, or knew, that it would end with a chapter like this.

When we got married, we made vows to each other — *"for better, for worse, for richer, for poorer, in sickness and in health, till death do us part."* And now, here I was, standing at the very edge of that vow — where love, life, and eternity meet.

We had everything in place for Shelly's recovery. Her bedroom was transformed into what could only be described as a private hospital suite — fully equipped for her comfort. There was an adjustable reclining bed, a constant oxygen supply, testing apparatus, medications, and even a small electronic bell she could ring if she needed help.

The right foods, fruits, and beverages were always available. Around her was a circle of care and love — myself, our son and daughter, and our foster daughter, Sammilyn, who is a practicing nurse. My sister Debbie, a retired nurse with twenty-eight years of experience, stayed with us as well. Together, they ensured every detail was attended to. Another doctor lived two minutes away, and others were just a phone call off.

Friends, colleagues, and loved ones came often to visit. Shelly had touched so many lives — neighbours, students, lawmen, pastors and their spouses, church members, and especially the children she loved so dearly. Everywhere she worked, she left an imprint of kindness, humility, and joy. Everyone wanted her to get better. And since everything seemed perfectly set for her care, it was easy to believe that she would.

But her condition did not improve. Over time, her dependency on oxygen increased. Sleep became a struggle; lying flat in bed was no longer possible. She began to find creative ways to rest — sitting up in a wheelchair, leaning forward on a small bedside table. When her doctor, Dr. Susan Isaacs, realised how much this position comforted her, she asked her father to craft a wooden support with a makeshift pillow. That became Shelly's preferred way to sleep.

I could hardly bear to see her like that — day and night, gasping softly for air, too weak to speak. She was eating less, drinking less, and growing weaker by the day.

One afternoon, she tried to express how she felt. I couldn't hold back my tears. I went aside and wept bitterly. That same day, a pastor friend called and prayed with me. Peace returned, and I thanked God for restoring my calm.

Each time Shelly found it hard to breathe, she would ask us to increase the oxygen flow. We were advised that the less oxygen she depended on, the better her chances of recovery — but she would often glance at the gauge, then whisper, *"Turn it up a little more."* It broke my heart, knowing we were nearing the point where it could go no higher.

Then came the morning of November 7, 2025. Shelly requested the maximum oxygen level, but even at that, she was struggling terribly. We called her doctor, who advised that we summon the ambulance.

Shelly had often said she didn't want to suffer. Remembering her words, I stepped out of the room, told the Lord what she had said, and prayed simply, *"Your will be done."*

When I returned, I asked if she wanted to lie on the bed. She nodded gently, and we helped her settle in. The ambulance arrived soon after. She couldn't be taken out in a wheelchair this time — only on a stretcher. That, in itself, spoke volumes.

It was her final trip to the A&E Department of the Linden Hospital Complex — the same institution where she had worked faithfully for nine years, giving her best in service to others.

There she lay, breathing faintly, surrounded by family and colleagues. I sat by her side in a chair someone had provided for me, silently watching the woman I loved more than life itself. I had received a call forty-five minutes earlier from the internal medicine specialist — the kind of call no one wants to get — gently telling me not to expect a favourable outcome. But I didn't share that with anyone.

I stepped outside briefly because the room felt cold from the air conditioning. When I returned, I saw quiet movements and heard soft whispers. Then I noticed the change — the stillness.

A nurse approached me and said softly, *"She's gone."*

I was asked to close her eyes, and with trembling hands, I did. Tears streamed down my face as others around me wept and held me close in comfort.

The woman I had met, loved, married, and lived with for thirty-seven years had gone home to be with the Lord. We had not parted through violence, neglect, or divorce — but through the pure fulfilment of our vows: *"Till death do us part."*

Thirty-seven years of Bliss, Blisters, and Blessings had come to an end — not in despair, but in destiny. We did not separate for any reason, because we were truly Rightly Wed and Groomed.

Reflection & Devotion – Love's Lasting Flame

Death could not erase what love built.

For those who walk this road—watching someone they love slip away while clinging to faith—know this: God's grace walks with you even there. When words fail and prayers turn into tears, the Holy Spirit interprets every sigh.

*"Precious in the sight of the Lord is the death
of his saints."*

— Psalm 116:15 (KJV)

Shelly's passing was not the end of our love story — it was the continuation of God's story through us. Heaven gained a song that once sang beside me, and though my days now echo differently, the melody of her love remains.

Love does not end at the grave. It transcends it. It continues in the faith we keep, the memories we hold, and the lives we touch because of the love we once received.

*"Who shall separate us from the love of
Christ? ... Neither death, nor life ... shall be
able to separate us from the love of God,
which is in Christ Jesus our Lord."*

— Romans 8:35–39 (KJV)

So, as I close this final chapter, I do so not in sorrow, but in gratitude — for thirty-seven years of love that was tested, refined, and sealed by grace.

And though the bed beside me is now empty, my heart is full — for love, once rightly wed and groomed, never dies.

Final Blessing

As we bring this book to a close, I offer a heartfelt prayer and blessing to every couple, every reader, and every seeker of enduring love.

May your marriage be clothed with grace, girded with strength, and seasoned with laughter. May your love weather every storm and soar on every breeze of joy. When the days grow long and the nights uncertain, may you remember your vows—not just the words you said, but the hearts that spoke them.

Let your home be a sanctuary, not of perfection, but of peace—where kindness outlasts conflict, where forgiveness finds its voice, and where God is always welcome.

To those newlywed, may your foundation be firm and your joy full.

To those bruised by years, may healing come like rain.

To the hopeless, may a flicker rise again.

To the strong, keep building, keep blooming.

As Shelly and I had lived and learnt, so can you.

Let love be your legacy. Let faith be your fuel.

And may you, too, be rightly wed and lovingly groomed.

With love and grace,

Pastor Walter "Spere" Lewis

Linden, Guyana

In Loving Memory of Shelly Lewis

(June 18, 1968 – November 7, 2025)

Beloved wife, devoted mother, faithful servant of God.

Your life was a song of grace — gentle, steadfast, and true.

You loved deeply, gave freely, and served humbly.

You faced pain with courage, faith, and laughter, teaching us that beauty remains even in brokenness.

Though your voice is silent, its echo lingers in every heart you touched, every smile you inspired, and every prayer you prayed.

You were, and will forever be, my partner, my joy, my answered prayer— Rightly Wed and Groomed for this life and the life to come.

> *"Her children arise and call her blessed; her husband also, and he praises her."*

> *— Proverbs 31:28 (NIV)*

Until we meet again — I will keep the flame of our love burning bright, trusting that God, who joined us in time, will reunite us in eternity.

> *— Pastor Walter "Spere" Lewis*

About the Author

Pastor Walter *"Spere"* Lewis is a seasoned minister of the Gospel, marriage counsellor, and spiritual father to many. With over two decades of service in Christian ministry, he brings not only theological depth but also heartfelt authenticity to his work with couples and families.

Hailing from the vibrant town of Linden, Guyana—a place filled with hills and valleys, river-front, warm community bonds, and rich spiritual heritage—Pastor Spere is known for his unique blend of practical wisdom and spiritual insight. He has served faithfully as the Senior Pastor of Fruits of Calvary AOG church, where he champions the cause of healthy marriages and strong families.

Married to Shelburn *"Shelly"* Lewis for 37 years, their union has weathered seasons of bliss, blisters, and blessings. Their journey, marked by love, laughter, trials, and triumphs, is the beating heart of this book.

Pastor Spere is also the visionary behind the *"Rightly Wed & Groomed"* Marriage Celebration, a signature vow renewal event designed to rekindle love and restore joy in marriages. He is a sought-after counsellor of both young and older couples, and those seeking to get married, offering biblical guidance and empathetic support rooted in his own lived experiences.

A father, grandfather, mentor, and man of faith—he remains committed to helping couples discover the divine joy of doing life together God's way. Through this book, he extends that ministry to the wider world, believing that every marriage can be Rightly Wed & Groomed with grace, intentionality, and God at the centre.